CONFLICT
under
Control

CONFLICT under Control

JEFF NEWMAN

REGULAR BAPTIST PRESS
3715 N Ventura Dr
Arlington Heights, IL 60004

CONFLICT UNDER CONTROL
© 2007 Regular Baptist Press • Schaumburg, Illinois
All rights reserved. Printed in U.S.A.
www.RegularBaptistPress.org • 1-800-727-4440
RBP5363 • ISBN: 978-1-59402-652-2

Second printing—2009

Contents

	Preface 7
Lesson 1	What Is the Goal of Conflict? 9
Lesson 2	Who Is God? 19
Lesson 3	Who Are Other People? 29
Lesson 4	What Do I Think? 39
Lesson 5	How Do I Respond? 49
Lesson 6	What Must I Do? 57
Lesson 7	Who Are My Examples? 67
	Afterword 75
	Answers 77

PREFACE

As a result of sin's entrance into the world, we live on a broken planet. We live around and with fallen, broken people, and we ourselves are fallen and broken. Although Christ has removed the enslaving hold of sin in our lives, the sin in us—with its disposition against God—still remains our greatest enemy and source of conflict.

None of us can avoid the presence of conflicts in our lives:
- Brothers and sisters fight over toys.
- Teenagers argue with their parents over curfew.
- Husbands and wives disagree about how to use the family finances.
- Employees complain about their bosses.
- Employers complain about their employees.
- A church member misinterprets another's actions.
- Political parties fight for control of government.

The Bible describes our world of conflict with great precision, because the God of the Bible knows His creation. Yet the Scriptures go beyond an accurate description of conflict to provide rich answers to people in the midst of the conflicts. These answers do not come to us in the form of a checklist for conflict resolution. They do not come as a mere skill set that we need to develop to get along better with people.

No, these answers come in the form of a Person—the Lord Jesus Christ. This is good news—the best news. Why? Because what is wrong with us goes deeper than problems that can be solved with mere skills. What is wrong with us goes to the very heart of who we are, and Christ is the only One Who can, by His Spirit, produce the change of heart we need to live for His glory.

Paul clearly saw this truth in his own life and in the lives of those around him. For example, in Philippians 4:1–10 Paul disclosed a conflict between Euodias and Syntyche and urged the women to have the same mind in the Lord. He also called on the church members to help Euodias and Syntyche resolve their differences. The inspired words of Scripture to this church will help us to depend on Christ when we face the conflicts of life in this fallen world. The wisdom of Scripture applied to our lives will cause us to rejoice in the God Who understands and changes us.

Lesson 1
What Is the Goal of Conflict?

Imagine the scene.

The news has spread among the believers in the city of Philippi: "Epaphroditus, our pastor, has returned. He brought a letter from Paul!"

The Letter Is Read

The believers have gathered together, and the letter is being read aloud. Sounds of rejoicing fill the room when the believers hear, "I thank my God upon every remembrance of you, always in every prayer of mine for you all making request with joy" (Philippians 1:3, 4).

Paul's report of the spread of the gospel even while he was imprisoned encourages the Philippians' hearts.

> But I would ye should understand, brethren, that the things

which happened unto me have fallen out rather unto the furtherance of the gospel; so that my bonds in Christ are manifest in all the palace, and in all other places; and many of the brethren in the Lord, waxing confident by my bonds, are much more bold to speak the word without fear. (Philippians 1:12–14)

A few words later, the Philippians' thoughts turn to their walk with God—rejoicing in His work in their lives and sorrowing over their failures to live out the life of Christ—as they hear:

Look not every man on his own things, but every man also on the things of others. Let this mind be in you, which was also in Christ Jesus: Who, being in the form of God, thought it not robbery to be equal with God: But made himself of no reputation, and took upon him the form of a servant, and was made in the likeness of men: And being found in fashion as a man, he humbled himself, and became obedient unto death, even the death of the cross. (Philippians 2:4–8)

They smile with anticipation as they hear of Paul's intentions to send Timothy, their brother in Christ, for a visit. Those who know him can already see his face and hear his voice. Others look forward to meeting this man of God who engendered such love among their friends in the assembly (Philippians 2:19–22).

1. Read Philippians 2:25–30.

   a. How might you have felt as you read these words about your faithful pastor, Epaphroditus, who had recently returned from his long visit with Paul?

   It would have felt good that someone cared that much

   b. What would you have said to your pastor after reading these words?

   that I'm praying for him.

As you view the scene of the Philippians reading their letter from Paul, you might see a tear or two fall from the eyes of many as they hear about their pastor's illness and his dedication to Paul and to God. Some are inwardly embarrassed that they have questioned their pastor's loyalty to them during his long absence. The facial expressions and words spoken quietly to Epaphroditus in that moment bring joy to the congregation (Philippians 2:25–30).

As the reading continues, the room falls silent. Everyone is contemplating Paul's intense words of warning: "Beware of dogs, beware of evil workers, beware of the concision" (Philippians 3:2).

Some are uneasy with Paul's words. "Are these people really as bad as Paul is saying?" they whisper. Others nod their heads knowingly as the alarming words are read. "This part of the letter warrants further study and meditation," they remark. They know that Paul's words are calling them to personal watchfulness and change for God's glory and the benefit of their unity.

2. Read Philippians 4:1–13.

    a. What additional responses would you have seen and heard in the room as these verses were read?

    b. How would you have felt?

Through his letter, Paul has brought into the open the quarrel that everyone knows about, but that has gone unresolved for so long. Paul has called on the church to get involved and help Euodias and Syntyche resolve their disagreement—to become of the same mind in the Lord. Maybe it seems as if ignoring the conflict has worked, as their outward conflict has quieted down. Maybe everyone has given up trying because the effort doesn't seem worth the frustration. For whatever reason, Paul, under the direction of the Spirit of God, has brought the need to resolve this conflict back to the forefront of everyone's mind.

3. What reasons, other than those already mentioned, do people give for failing to deal with conflict?

As the remainder of Paul's letter is read, some of the Philippians barely hear his words of thanks for the financial gift they sacrificed to collect and send with Epaphroditus. Even the greetings sent from believers in the household of the Roman emperor Caesar seem to register only briefly in the thoughts of some in the assembly (Philippians 4:10–23). Many of them likely have their thoughts captured with Euodias and Syntyche and all of the what-ifs of the task before them. "How can we encourage these two women to be of the same mind in the Lord?"

Christ Is the Answer to Conflict

From our earliest days on this earth, we have contributed to and experienced conflict. Remember: conflict is inevitable as we fallen, broken people live in a fallen, broken world, surrounded by other fallen, broken people. Maybe you are in the midst of a conflict now. Are you involved in a disagreement with another person? Have you been called on to assist others in resolving a conflict? From the very beginning of his letter, Paul drew the attention of the Philippians to the only Person Who could move Euodias and Syntyche toward restoration—the Lord Jesus Christ.

4. Read Philippians 2:1–4. Record the first command that Paul gave to his readers in these verses.

Fulfill or complete, Paul's joy becoming like-minded.

Paul called on his readers to bring completeness to his joy. In their union with Christ, God's children find encouragement. In Christ's love, God's children find comfort. On the basis of His indwelling Spirit, God's children share fellowship. In Christ, God's children find tenderness and compassionate mercy.

5. Reread Philippians 2:3 and 4. In what ways could the Philippians bring completeness to Paul's joy?

By not acting in selfishness or pride

Paul's words to the Philippians call us to give ourselves to the work of unity. If unity is to be achieved, we must have some foundational commitments. Likewise, if the Philippians were to encourage Euodias and Syntyche to have the mind of Christ, they themselves needed to strive to become like-minded. They needed to commit themselves to a self-sacrificing, others-focused love. They needed to dedicate themselves to becoming one in affection and one in thought. They needed to refuse self-promotion, but rather to humble themselves.

6. Consider a recent conflict that you have experienced. How did you demonstrate the commitments discussed above in the midst of the conflict?

7. Where did you fail to demonstrate these commitments? Be thoughtful and specific.

Where you have failed, confess that sin to God, rejoice in God's forgiveness, and commit yourself to new obedience.

8. Read Philippians 2:5.

    a. What command must be followed if conflicts are to be faced in a godly manner?

    b. Compare this command to Paul's words in Philippians 4:2. What goal did Paul hold out for Euodias and Syntyche?

Conflicts Provide Opportunities to Become like Christ

Paul called on the Philippians to involve themselves in the conflict between Euodias and Syntyche because of the person and work of Christ. He knew that Euodias and Syntyche could restore their relationship with each other because Christ had already restored their relationship with God. Paul knew that all of the members of the church would grow in Christlikeness as they gave themselves to the task of assisting the women to be of the same mind in the Lord.

In the midst of any conflict, our goal must be to become more like Christ—to have the mind of Christ. Having the mind of Christ means that we give effort to understanding our lives and circumstances from His perspective. We strive to know His Word and live in the energy of His Spirit. Paul knew that for the Philippians to deal effectively with conflict, they would need to make it their goal to become more like Christ. As they helped Euodias and Syntyche resolve their conflict, they needed to see and live life from His perspective.

9. Read Philippians 2:5–11. What characteristic and works of Christ do these verses emphasize?

Characteristic

Works

Christlike humility

To respond properly in the face of conflicts, God's children must possess Christlike humility. Christ willingly veiled His glory, laid aside the independent exercise of all He shared with His Father, and became Man. In humility, Jesus Christ became forever undiminished deity and perfect humanity united in one person. In humility, Christ not only became a man, He became a servant—a bond slave doing the will of His Father and willingly serving others by becoming their perfect sacrifice for sin. Humility asks, "What is God's will? What will bring glory to Him? How can I serve others?" Pride declares, "I don't deserve to be treated this way. I want my way."

Christlike obedience

Christ's humility resulted in His perfect obedience. In conflict, we must give ourselves to submissive obedience to Him, the One Who deserves our full loyalty. In His humble allegiance to His Father, Jesus Christ, the Eternal One, submitted Himself to death. This fact alone should amaze us, but Christ's humility resulted in obedience to a death of utter humiliation reserved for the worst of the offenders of His time. If we make Christlikeness our goal as we face conflict, we will refuse to respond with words of sinful anger.

We will not seek to persuade people to our points of view, but we will rather pray, speak, and act in ways that seek to lead people to God's perspective. We will refuse to give in to the temptation to make the conflict be about ourselves and our reputations. Instead we will commit ourselves to obeying the One Who made Himself of no reputation.

10. Read James 1:1–12. What does God promise to those who meet the trials and temptations of this life with humble obedience?

Christ's humble obedience demonstrated His trust in His Father, and His Father honored the obedience of His beloved Son. Our God is trustworthy. If we fail to trust God in conflict, we will be forced to trust fully in ourselves or others. Trusting anyone more than God always results in disappointment. That disappointment may lead to a fear and anxiety that controls us, or it may lead to all sorts of sinful responses toward other people. However, when we make Christlikeness our goal in conflict, we are demonstrating trust in Christ. Trusting Him will bring obedient peace in the midst of conflict, and in the end, it will bring reward from God.

11. Consider a recent conflict that you experienced. How did you demonstrate the mind of Christ through humility, obedience, and trust in God? Rejoice in God's work in your life.

12. Where did you fail to demonstrate the mind of Christ through humility, obedience, and trust in God?

Rejoice in God's work that reveals these sins to you through His Word. Confess to God these failures as sin, and commit yourself to renewed obedience. Resist the temptation to weaken your confession with any blame shifting.

13. Read Philippians 4:1–9. What key themes and commands do you notice as Paul instructed the Philippians concerning Euodias and Syntyche?

In the remainder of this study, we will direct our attention to Paul's instruction to the believers at Philippi to involve themselves with Euodias and Syntyche in helping them be of the same mind in the Lord. Paul emphasized four themes that will become the focus of our study. First, Paul emphasized the character and work of God. Second, Paul emphasized seeing others from God's perspective. Third, Paul emphasized correct thinking in the midst of conflict. And finally, Paul emphasized the personal responsibilities of obedience in conflict.

Ask God to teach you from His Word as we study His will for us in the midst of life's conflicts. When necessary, confess your failure to handle conflicts in a Christlike manner. Commit yourself afresh to making your own growth in Christlikeness the goal. Rejoice that God makes sense out of the conflicts we experience and that He gives us wonderful ways to respond in the energy of the Spirit of His Son—responses that result in our growth in Christlikeness.

LESSON 2
WHO IS GOD?

Hello. This—" As she answered the phone, Mary did not even complete her greeting before she recognized the sobs of her friend Joanne on the other end of the line. "What's wrong, Joanne?" Mary quickly asked.

"I'm so angry and hurt that I don't know what to do," came the reply. "I've worked so hard at coordinating the banquet for our missions conference, and now I find out that Kelly has been complaining to the other ladies about the decorations and food. She even told Lucy that I really didn't care about missions, but just wanted attention for myself. Mary, you know I love our missionaries. How could she say such a thing?"

    1. a. What might people say to Joanne in this situation?

       b. What would you say to Joanne?

2. What themes or truths of Scripture come to mind that could help Mary face this situation in a Christlike way?

God's Character and Work

When the Holy Spirit directed Paul to bring up the conflict between Euodias and Syntyche, Paul did not begin by offering advice on problem solving or conflict resolution. He did not begin with techniques or skills. He did not even begin with bringing out the details of the conflict.

3. Read Philippians 4:1 and 2. What did Paul emphasize as he brought the conflict between Euodias and Syntyche into the open?

Do you see where Paul began? He began by drawing the Philippians' attention to their relationship with God and with one another. He continued this emphasis throughout all of his instructions to them. In this lesson, we will consider what Paul said about God. In the next lesson, we will turn our attention to Paul's reminders to the Philippian believers about their relationships with one another.

4. Why do you think Paul began by reminding the Philippians of the character and work of God?

In conflict, we are tempted to make the consideration of ourselves our central theme. When we give in to this temptation, the conflict becomes all about us—our desires, our perspectives, our way, our reputations. We might not admit this focus to others or even to ourselves, but our thoughts, words, and actions betray that it is true. This temptation not only befalls those who are involved in the conflict, but it also ensnares those who seek to help others resolve their conflicts. Our own reputations, the investment of time, the frustration over little or slow progress, along with a host of other distractions, compete to divert our attention away from God.

Paul began by directing attention to God. He knew that if Euodias and Syntyche were to become more like Christ as they sought to be of the same mind in the Lord, they would need to fix their attention on the God they were called to emulate. In addition, the members of the church needed to make God's will and reputation central in their quest to help Euodias and Syntyche. In the midst of every conflict, we must begin in this same place. Whether it is a moment of disagreement between a husband and wife or a longstanding conflict between two church members, God's goal—His will and reputation—must become and continue to be the desire of everyone involved in seeking to bring resolution to the conflict.

5. Read Philippians 4:1–9. Note the ways in which Paul emphasized the character and work of God. What did Paul say or imply about God in each of these verses?

    Verse 1

    Verse 2

    Verse 4

    Verse 5

Verse 6

Verses 7, 9

Stability, Unity, and Joy

6. How do people attempt to produce stability and achieve unity in the midst of conflict? Consider both right and wrong methods.

Right methods

Wrong methods

Paul began by reminding the Philippians that the Lord was the source of their stability. He alone provided them with a firm foundation that never failed to bring stability in the midst of utter chaos. As we stand firm on Christ, we will find the strength to remain steadfast and faithful in the midst of the conflicts of this fallen, broken world.

7. Read the passages in the chart on page 23. How do they picture the steadfastness of God? How do they draw your focus to Him—His will and His desires? What do they teach you about God's stability?

Passage	Picture	Focus	God's Stability
Psalm 18:1–3			
Psalm 95:1–7			
Proverbs 30:5			
Romans 12:16–21			

Paul also reminded his readers that God was the source of their unity. He called on Euodias and Syntyche to find unity by having the mind of Christ—by seeking to understand themselves and their situation from His perspective. In conflict, we all too often make it our goal to persuade others to our point of view or to our course of action. We seek unity in other people's agreement with us. These goals blind us to the work of God in our lives. However, when all parties in the conflict work individually and then collectively to seek unity in the mind of Christ, He will produce unity in their hearts.

8. Read the following passages. What do they teach you about unity?

Psalm 133:1–3

Romans 12:9–21

Ephesians 4:1–16

9. Consider a recent conflict you have experienced. Where did you go to find stability? How did you seek to achieve unity?

10. a. What does this study teach you about your desires in the midst of the conflict?

   b. How have you been obedient? Rejoice in the Lord for your obedience.

   c. How have you been disobedient? Respond to God's call to repent.

After Paul reminded the Philippians that God is the source of enduring stability and unity, he reminded them that authentic joy comes from God alone: "Rejoice in the Lord alway: and again I say, Rejoice" (Philippians 4:4). When Paul made this statement, he was not radically changing the subject, turning his attention to another matter. In the midst of conflict, all people measure their joy according to a standard. Too often, hope waxes and wanes with the rising and falling prospects of resolving the conflict. Instead, our joy should come from our relationship with the Lord.

In times of conflict, as in all of life, everyone finds joy and purpose in someone or something. Some people take joy in getting their own way—in being right or in winning the argument. Some people find joy in the power they have over others who are impaired or paralyzed by conflict. Some people take joy in the emotional high that the warm feelings of unity bring to them. God wants us to find our joy in His work in our lives as He refines us.

11. a. What brings you the most joy in times of conflict?

b. How does this source of joy reflect your desires and goals in the midst of conflict?

God's Presence

"Let your moderation be known unto all men. The Lord is at hand" (Philippians 4:5). What happens when you are having an intense or angry conversation with a family member or coworker and the phone or the doorbell rings or the boss walks by? Exactly! Your whole demeanor changes. Your tone of voice becomes pleasant. You may even smile and laugh. Why? Because someone else's presence became more important to you than the goal of your previous words and tone of voice.

Paul reminded us that the Lord is the ever-present One and that His Son may return for His own at this very moment. As a result, our gentle treatment of others must not be motivated by our desire to better convince them to our point of view. No. We must be kind and gentle in our responses to others because God is with us.

12. Read Psalm 23. According to the psalmist, what does the presence of God in our lives provide for us?

13. Read the account of Peter's denial of Christ in Luke 22:54–62. How did the awareness of Christ's presence affect Peter?

The awareness of God's presence in our lives should change us. God's presence brings comfort and hope to His children. We can face any conflict with gentle obedience because God provides comfort in life's dark valleys. We can resist the desire to seek comfort and satisfaction in winning, but we can find our satisfaction in God's shepherding work in our own lives. God's presence also brings purity. When we remember that God is always present, we will submit ourselves to His work and His will in conflict.

14. a. To whom do people go for advice on resolving the conflicts they have with others?

b. Where do you go?

The ever-present God hears our prayers. "Be careful for nothing; but in every thing by prayer and supplication with thanksgiving let your requests be made known unto God" (Philippians 4:6). Paul reminded the Philippians that they should take all their anxieties to God with thanksgiving. God wants us to cry out to Him in the midst of the confusion and despair of conflict. Our prayers offered to Him with thanksgiving demonstrate our trust in Him and help change the focus of our hearts to His will for us.

15. a. What does Philippians 4:7 say will be the result of taking our anxieties to God in thankful prayer?

b. How does Philippians 4:9 expand this idea?

Peaceful conflict—the very idea could win a competition for the world's greatest oxymoron. Yet God says that His children can endure and resolve conflict with His peace. In the midst of conflict, everyone seeks refuge—a place of peace. Some turn for refuge to those who agree with them; some use work and hobbies to avoid facing the conflict; others escape with food, alcohol, or other drugs; some run away; some even commit murder or suicide. God calls on us to seek refuge in Him because His peace alone can guard the very center of our beings—our hearts and minds. His peace in times of conflict will lead us to seek counsel from His people who know His Word. His peace will lead us to cling to His desire for us and to grow in Christlikeness as we respond to conflicts with thankful trust in Him.

16. Read James 4:1. What does this verse teach about the source of conflicts, quarrels, and wars?

17. Read James 4:7 and 8. What do these verses teach about the solution to conflict?

James reinforced Paul's starting point in the midst of conflict. If we are to grow in Christlikeness as we face life's conflicts, we must turn from our own desires and fix our attention on the character and work of our God. He is the source of our stability and unity. He is ever-present. He hears our prayers and is the source of true peace. When we give ourselves to knowing and glorifying God during life's conflicts both large and small, we will set aside our own desires and submit ourselves to His desires. As a result, the God of peace will produce His peace in us, and we will seek to live at peace with others.

18. Consider your thoughts and actions in the midst of a recent conflict. Did they reflect submission to God? When did you allow your desires to become more important than pleasing Christ, resulting in sin against God and others?

Rejoice in your submission to God. Confess your sin to God and seek forgiveness from others where necessary.

19. What commitments to change must you make and keep? List them.

Lesson 3
Who Are Other People?

Did you ever have a nickname? People's nicknames sometimes reflect their physical characteristics. "Bean" earned his nickname because he was tall and skinny during his high school years. The quick but uncoordinated person might be dubbed "Flash." Some nicknames reflect other qualities of the person. "Brain" is sometimes the smartest student in the class. I once had a coworker whose nickname was "Toad." I never had the courage to ask him why. Personally, I did not see the resemblance in look or in character. Each of the names "Hulk," "Slim," "Punky," "Chunky," "Sparky," and "Sunshine" brings to our minds a picture of the person behind the nickname.

Some nicknames are complimentary; others are derogatory. Sometimes nicknames reveal more about the attitude of the giver of the nickname than they do about the receiver. However, all nicknames share one common feature: they often become a part of the person's identity. When you think about the person, the nickname and its significance always come to your mind.

The Right Perception of Others

1. Read Philippians 4:1–3. List the ways Paul described the believers at Philippi.

To interact with others in a manner that pleases the Lord, we must view others as God views them. As a result, Paul reminded the Philippians of their relationship to each other in God's sight.

In the midst of conflict we often make statements that evaluate another person. These statements become a part of our interpretation of the other person—the identity we give him or her. "She is always so stubborn." "What a malcontent." "He never listens." "They are so ignorant." "I can't believe he is such a crank." "She's not the brightest crayon in the box." Sometimes the statements are so heinous that they remain only in our thoughts. But at times, those heinous thoughts come out in hurtful words.

2. What words of evaluation influenced your thoughts and responses toward others involved in a recent conflict?

Our own evaluations often replace God's evaluation of the person. By the words Paul used in writing to the Philippians, he set a tone for his instruction concerning the conflict between Euodias and Syntyche. He reminded the Philippians of their shared identity in Christ—His work in them and their past work for Him.

A Shared Identity

First, Paul reminded the Philippians that in Christ they were related as spiritual brothers and sisters. By his simple use of the term "brethren" (4:1), he reminded the Philippians that they are eternally related to each other as family. They share the same Father. They share in the glory of His Son, and as a result, they had become His children.

When we call someone brother or sister, we are using a term of equality. We have a shared identity and position. Earthly brothers or sisters sometimes share rooms. They are called on to share toys and clothes. They often stick up for one another when no one else will. As eternal brothers and sisters, we who know Christ must share in the task of helping others become of the same mind in the Lord. When we do, all of us who are God's children become more like His Son—the One Who is not ashamed to be known as our Brother as we live for Him (Hebrews 2:9–11).

3. Read the passages listed on the chart. Note Paul's use of the term "brother." Why do you think Paul chose to address his readers with that term? What can you learn from this designation as you face the conflicts in your life?

Passage	What You Can Learn
Galatians 6:1, 2	
Philippians 1:12–18	
2 Thessalonians 3:11–16	
Philemon 10–21	

A Godly Love

Next Paul described the Philippian believers as people he deeply loved (Philippians 4:1). He called them beloved, his joy, and his crown. Paul reminded them that his self-sacrificing love for them had moved him to bring the gospel to them and to invest and endanger his life on their behalf (see Acts 16:12–40). His profound love for them drove him to desire to see them and spend time with them. Paul received joy from the Philippians' relationship with the Lord, and he reminded them that his work on their behalf would bring him eternal reward.

When we are engaged in conflict with a fellow believer, we often fail to honor the sacrifices of the ones God used in bringing the other person to Himself. When we make the conflict all about getting our own way, we disregard God's love for others. We also disregard the love of those God has used to help others in their walk with Him. God wants conflicts to become an occasion for us to evaluate our love for others. He wants our conflicts to become avenues for us to see His love toward us and for us to show His love to others. In the midst of the conflict, as we treat others as beloved of God, we will become more like Christ. We will seek to respond according to His Word, rather than according to our own will.

4. Notice the use of "beloved" in the passages below. Record the writer's message and how his use of "beloved" might have influenced the reader's reception of the message.

Passage	Writer's Message	Reception
2 Corinthians 7:1		
Philippians 2:12–16		
2 Peter 3:1–4, 13–18		

5. Evaluate yourself. In recent conflicts, did your words and actions demonstrate that you saw other believers as brothers and sisters in Christ?

6. a. Did your words and actions demonstrate that you saw other believers as beloved?

    b. How might your words and actions have differed if you had viewed the other person from these perspectives?

    c. Do you need to confess any sin to God?

    d. From whom do you need to seek forgiveness?

    e. What new commitments of obedience should you make?

Fellow Laborers

Third, Paul reminded the Philippians that they shared the identity of being fellow laborers (Philippians 4:3). These few words caused the Philippians to stop and think of all the exhausting efforts they had shared in their work for God's church at Philippi. The fact that they had worked beside each other for God's glory in the past was to motivate them to work toward unity for His glory in the future—even though at that time they were opposing each other.

Camaraderie often grows from shared goals and shared effort. These shared goals and energies ought to result in a shared commitment to our fellow laborers. A severed relationship between those who have toiled side by side in the Lord's work should always bring grief. A commitment to our coworkers in Christ ought to motivate us to work at resolving our differences in a Christlike manner.

7. Consider 1 Corinthians 3:1–10.

   a. What did Paul call the Corinthian Christians as a result of their selfish approach to conflict?

   b. How did he expose to them the error of their desires, thoughts, and actions?

8. What parallels do you see to Philippians 4?

The Book of Life

9. Read the following passages. What do they teach you about the Book of Life?

   Revelation 20:11–15

   Revelation 21:10–27

Finally, Paul reminded the Philippians that together their names are in the Book of Life for all time and eternity (Philippians 4:3). They share the same relationship, the same purpose, and the same destiny. When we face conflicts with fellow believers, we must remind ourselves that we share a relationship with the God of the universe, and we share an eternal destiny. His glory will be fully revealed in us when we are together in His presence. As a result, we must make His glory our primary concern now. When we remind ourselves that the names of all of God's children are recorded in His Book of Life, we will move humbly toward the ones with whom we will share eternity.

Unbelievers

10. Read Genesis 1:26 and James 3:8–10. What statement of identity is made about all mankind?

11. Read the following verses and summarize what they say about Christ, mankind, and sin.

   1 John 2:1, 2

   2 Peter 2:1

In Philippians 4 Paul dealt with a problem between two believers. Yet many times our conflicts involve unbelievers. Even then—especially then—we need to see all people from God's perspective. Every human being is created in His image. His Son shed His life's blood for the sins of all mankind. God sees all mankind from this perspective. So must we.

If God's love for the people of the world, created in His image, caused Him to send His Son to die, then we must be willing to sacrifice to show His love to others. Our love for all mankind ought to drive us to treat everyone with love and respect. It ought to cause us to be longsuffering toward unbelievers who wrong us. It ought to humble us so that we are willing to acknowledge to unbelievers our sins against them. It ought to drive us to emulate the God Who is "not willing that any should perish, but that all should come to repentance" (2 Peter 3:9).

12. Consider a recent conflict you have had that involved unbelievers. How did your actions reflect that you treated them as individuals created in the image of God for whom Christ died?

13. Where did you fail to show forth God's love?

Rejoice in God's work in your life. Turn from any sin and begin to treat others in new, more Christlike ways.

The way God sees and evaluates people must become our way of seeing and evaluating others. When we strive to see others as God sees them, we will see people as created in the image of God. We will remember that Christ died for the sins of all mankind. We will remind ourselves that as believers, we share the same relationship, purpose, and destiny. When we seek to see others from God's perspective, His Word will then become the standard by which we evaluate our own actions and the actions of others. As a result, we will grow in Christlikeness in the midst of the conflicts of life in this fallen, broken world.

14. Make a list of the people with whom you spend most of your time. What words of Scripture help you see these people as God sees them? Write your responses following their names.

LESSON 4
WHAT DO I THINK?

Paul captured the attention of the Philippians with the grace of God at work in them: God gives stability and unity; He lavishes joy on His children; He is always near; He listens when His children cry out to Him; He imparts peace; God had brought the Philippians into eternal relationship with each other on the basis of His Son's death and resurrection.

God produced in Paul a love for the Philippians that motivated him to spend his life for them and others. Through His grace, God enabled the Philippian believers to labor together, and by God's grace, their names were forever recorded in the Book of Life. Paul desired for these reminders to become the Philippians' foundation as they sought to help Euodias and Syntyche be of the same mind in the Lord.

A Spinning Mind

Listen to your thoughts. Where does your mind drift when you lift anchor and allow it to sail wherever your heart takes it? What captures your thoughts? At times, we allow ourselves to think whatever we want to think without measuring our thoughts according to God's standard. Always our thoughts reflect the desires of our hearts (Hebrews 4:12). When we desire to become more like Christ, our thoughts turn to Him and to His Word. We may even find it necessary to argue with ourselves, combating our wrong thinking with the truth we know from God's Word. Whatever our thoughts, these meditations both reflect our hearts and become the interpretations through which we view our lives. In the midst of conflict, we must guard our thoughts if we are to grow to become more like our Savior.

1. What command did Paul give in Philippians 4:8?

"Faith" Thinking

Paul commanded the Philippian believers to think properly in the midst of conflict. He wanted them to give careful attention to their thoughts to ensure that their interpretation of their lives and circumstances matched God's way of viewing life. To help them do this, Paul provided several characteristics to consider as they evaluated their thoughts. Before we consider these characteristics, we need to explore the type of careful thinking in which we are called to engage, especially when we face conflicts.

Abraham

2. Read Hebrews 11:17–19. (You may also want to read Genesis 22:1–14.) As Abraham considered God's command to offer Isaac, what reasoned conclusion did he come to, according to verse 19?

3. How would you describe this type of thinking?

When God commanded Abraham to take his son and offer him as a sacrifice, Abraham faced a dilemma. God had promised that He would raise up a great nation through Isaac, but God was instructing Abraham to kill Isaac before fulfilling His promise. What false conclusions might Abraham have come to as he pondered the promise and the command?

Abraham might have concluded that God had gone back on His promise. Or Abraham might have thought that God had not really meant what He said when He commanded the offering of Isaac. Yet Abraham believed both God's promise and God's command. He came to the only conclusion to which the thoughts of faith could lead him—God would resurrect Isaac from the dead after Abraham offered him. Abraham could never have reached this conclusion without the careful reasoning that his faith demanded.

Paul

4. Read Philippians 3:13 and 14. As Paul responded to his past, what did he conclude based on his careful thought?

Paul, like Abraham, considered the matter before him. Based on his thoughtful deliberation, Paul resolved that he must disregard his past successes and failures. He then concluded that He must pursue the reward that comes from knowing and pleasing Christ. This reasoned conclusion became the interpretation that drove his response to God and to others.

5. In what ways does the thinking of Abraham and Paul challenge you as you consider the thoughts that spin in your mind when you experience conflict?

When the writer of Hebrews said that Abraham offered up Isaac "accounting that God was able to raise him up, even from the dead," he was referring to the same type of thinking that Paul described in Philippians 4:8. Seeing with the eyes of faith will lead us to think God's thoughts in the midst of conflict. We dare not allow our own desires to become the source of the evaluations and interpretations we cling to. Instead, we must carefully consider ourselves, others, and our circumstances—all from God's perspective.

Characteristics for Evaluating Thoughts

6. Choose an antonym (a word that is the opposite of the word) for each of the words from Philippians 4:8 listed below. Write your answer next to the Biblical word. If you have difficulty thinking of one word, use a sentence or phrase that gives the opposite meaning of the word.

True

Honest

Just

Pure

Lovely

Of good report

Virtuous

Praiseworthy

Did you find question 6 difficult? I did. Thinking is no easy task, and the simple exercise above did not have the intensity of concern and emotion that comes with thinking in the midst of conflict. As a result, we must evaluate our thinking based on the characteristics Paul outlined in Philippians 4:8. When we do this, we will see our conflicts through the sharp lens of God's Word, rather than through the blurred, even darkened, lenses of our own desires.

Thinking That Reflects God's Holiness

Paul first called on the Philippians to engage in thinking that reflected the holiness of God. He called on them to think **true** thoughts—thoughts in harmony with the facts. He instructed them to engage in **honest** thinking. Paul also said that the Philippians should think in ways that **reflect honor** (or are **"just"**). For example, if someone read a transcript of the Philippians' thoughts, that person should have found their thoughts above reproach. The Philippians' thoughts should have led them to contemplate their just God and evaluate themselves—and others—from His righteous perspective. Paul reminded the Philippians that their thoughts should reflect their position in Christ. God declared them holy on the basis of their faith in the finished work of Christ, and they were to think on things **pure** and holy.

Dwelling on true, honest, just, and pure thoughts in the midst of conflict will change our focus. Instead of jumping to conclusions, we will carefully consider the facts. We will separate the facts from our *interpretation* of the facts. We will measure our thoughts according to God's Word, not according to our own standards, which become skewed by the desires of our flesh. As we make it our goal to yield to God's work of sanctification—making us more like Christ—we will turn from our own ways of evaluating ourselves, others, and our circumstances. Instead, we will submit to God's perspective provided for us in His Word.

7. Consider a recent conflict you have experienced. Evaluate your thoughts. Where did they reflect the type of thinking Paul commanded—true, honest, just, and pure thinking? Rejoice in God's work in you.

8. Where did your thoughts fail to measure up to these characteristics? Be specific in your evaluation. Confess your sin to God. Rejoice in His forgiveness.

9. How should your thoughts change? What must you stop thinking? What must you begin to think?

Thoughts That Reflect Love for Others

Paul next used words that drew the Philippians to think the best, not the worst. He led them to ask, "Are my thoughts **lovely**?" Paul desired that the Philippians think thoughts that would bring delight. He wanted them to think thoughts of kindness. He next reminded the Philippians that they should think thoughts of **good report**. They were to carefully guard their thoughts so they would think thoughts of respect for others. Paul called on them to think **virtuous thoughts**—thoughts that are excellent in character. Finally, he concluded his list of the characteristics of proper thinking with **praiseworthy thoughts.** He asked the Philippians to consider whether their thoughts brought praise to God.

10. Read 1 Corinthians 13:4–8. In the chart on page 45, list the similarities you see between this list of the characteristics of

love and the characteristics of the thinking Paul described in Philippians 4:8.

Characteristic in 1 Corinthians 13	Characteristic in Philippians 4:8

11. Contemplate the same conflict you considered in question 7. Evaluate your thoughts. Where did they reflect lovely, respectful, virtuous, praiseworthy thinking? Rejoice in God's work in you. Once again, be specific in your evaluation.

12. Where did your thoughts fail to meet these standards? Confess your sin to God. Rejoice in His forgiveness.

13. How should your thoughts change? What must you stop thinking? What must you begin to think?

Results of Right Thinking

Paul called on believers to think thoughts characterized by holiness and love. This type of thinking produces three effects in the midst of conflicts. First, when we obey this command, we will refuse to allow our minds to wander aimlessly from thought to thought. We will refuse to allow our thoughts to drift to the worst-case scenarios or what-if fears. Second, we will not think more highly of ourselves than we ought to think. Rather, we will evaluate ourselves from God's perspective. Finally, we will judge the words and actions of others based on the truth of the Word of God, not based on our own personal agendas and goals. Responding to conflict in a Christlike way demands wise and loving discernment.

14. Read the passages below and summarize the truth of each one. Consider the Scriptures in light of the paragraph above.

2 Corinthians 10:5

Matthew 6:34

Romans 12:3

Once again, notice that the characteristics of proper thinking that we have studied in this lesson reflect the character of God. God is true, honest, and just, and He is indeed holy. Christ is altogether lovely, spotless, and worthy of all of our praise. Because of Christ, we can think in these ways and become more like Him through the work of His Spirit in us. When we stand before Him, submissive to His goal for us—Christlikeness—He produces in us by His grace the ability to think His thoughts. This wonderful transformation often takes place in the midst of the conflicts of this fallen, broken world. As we continue to respond submissively to Christ's work in us, we will grow to be more like Him.

15. Take some time to consider how God has changed you through His Word. How has your study of His Word in these lessons helped you to become more like Christ in the conflicts you are currently experiencing?

LESSON 5
HOW DO I RESPOND?

"What can I do to solve this problem? Now!" In conflict, we often jump quickly to an action plan for solving the problem. Yet when our plan of action becomes the focus, we may fail to approach conflicts in the ways that Philippians has instructed us so far. What have we learned?

First, we must submit ourselves to God's work of remaking us into the image of His Son. He uses conflicts as one of His tools to produce His holiness in us. When we see conflicts from this perspective, we will not view resolution of the conflict as the supreme goal, but rather as the result of the Christlike responses of all of those involved in the conflict. When God's children react with humble Christlike obedience in the midst of conflict, harmony results.

Second, we will rejoice in God's work in us and will always remember that His reputation and glory must remain our supreme pursuit. God provides stability in the instabilities of life. He produces unity in His yielded children. He gives abundant joy. The ever-present One hears ours prayers and bestows on us His peace in the midst of the world of chaos.

Third, Paul's reminders of the Philippians' shared identity encourage us to respond to others based on God's view of them and not our own. God and His Word must control our interpretations of others. We share a family relationship with our brothers and sisters in Christ. God and others have invested their love in these people. We have worked together for God's glory. We belong to God.

Fourth, this proper view of God and others provides a foundation for the remainder of our thoughts. These thoughts reflect the desires of our hearts, and our interpretations of life hold significant influence over our responses in the midst of conflict. Therefore, we must alter our thinking by turning from our own thoughts to the God Who transforms the thoughts and intents of our hearts.

1. Review your answer to the final question of the last lesson. Does your answer reflect changes in your behavior as well as changes in your thoughts and goals? If so, why do you think this is the case?

The Fruit of God's Work in Us

As you have submitted yourself to God's work, you are already seeing fruit from God's instructions borne out in your life even though we have yet to study Paul's commands for obedient action. This fruit-bearing reminds us of a very important truth: our greatest need in the midst of conflict is not a checklist for conflict resolution or skills of communication. Our greatest need is a Person—the Lord Jesus Christ—and our need to maintain a submissive heart before Him.

2. Read Luke 6:43–45.

   a. What does this passage teach you about the true source of your responses in the midst of conflict?

   b. From what source do your words originate?

   c. As a result, what then must change so you will respond to conflicts in a Christlike manner?

Exactly. We need a change of heart—a transformation of motives and desires—to successfully respond to conflicts. As we turn from our own fleshly desires to submit to God's will for us, we will act in ways that reflect God's character. We will seek to respond to conflicts in a manner that pleases Him. But when we fail to guard our hearts, we will find ourselves pursuing our own selfish goals even in the midst of our attempts to obey God.

Having established the foundational truths reviewed above, Paul then turned to the Philippians' responses in the midst of the conflicts of life. He did not begin with their actions because he was aiming for something higher than temporary behavioral change or short-term resolution of the conflict. He began with these truths because he knew that God works in the midst of conflicts to capture the very hearts of His children. As the Philippians turned in faith to God and sought Him in the midst of conflict, Paul knew they would obey from hearts desiring to please God. From their hearts, they would sustain their obedience in the midst of conflict.

3. Read Philippians 4:4–7. List the three commands Paul gave in these verses.

The Command to Rejoice

Paul first commanded the Philippians to rejoice. Notice the intensity with which he made this command. He called on the Philippians to rejoice at all times. He also repeated the command for emphasis: "Again I say, Rejoice." No one could escape Paul's call to rejoice. Yet at first glance, Paul's call to rejoice surprises us. A call to mourn over an ongoing conflict between two sisters in Christ would seem more appropriate. However, when we view conflict from God's perspective, Paul's command to rejoice will capture our attention and spur us to search for reasons to rejoice in the midst of conflict.

4. Read 1 Peter 4:12–14. What reasons do we have for rejoicing when we are in the midst of conflicts that come because we are seeking to honor Christ?

When we face conflict because of our obedience to Christ (or in the midst of our obedience), we can rejoice because we share in the sufferings of Christ. Seen from God's perspective, rejoicing is a logical response to conflict. Seemingly senseless mistreatment viewed in the light of Christ's suffering will provide us with a stability that produces both calm rejoicing and growth in holiness in the midst of conflict.

5. Read Hebrews 12:5–11. What reasons do we have for rejoicing when God chastises us because our own sin has brought conflict, or our sin has complicated a conflict?

Even when we have caused or contributed to a conflict through our own sinfulness, we have cause for rejoicing. Our loving God has revealed our sin to us. His Son has already paid the penalty for our sin. His chastening invites us to come close to Him, rather than move away from Him. When we turn to Him, we find full, complete forgiveness and the restoration of our fellowship with Him. God transforms conflicts into tools of our sanctification. As we seek forgiveness from the people we have wronged and commit to respond in new ways, we partake in the holiness of God and reap the peaceable fruit of righteousness. This growth is possible in Christ, even if others do not respond properly to our repentant obedience.

6. Consider a recent conflict. Where should you have seen cause for rejoicing? Thank the Lord for His work in you.

Reputation for Gentleness

Paul next reminded the Philippians that they should have a reputation for gentleness. He called on the Philippians to live in such a way that people would recognize them as kind and courteous. The Philippians' words and actions should reflect pleasantness and reasonableness. In the midst of conflict, we should treasure a good reputation more than we prize our own way. When we do, we will bring glory to God as we respond to others with gentleness, preferring them before ourselves.

7. Read James 3:13–18. How does this passage expand your concept of gentleness?

James shared Paul's themes. God reveals our hearts to us through our words and actions as we evaluate them according to His Word. We deceive ourselves if we think that we can perpetuate conflict and at the same time live in harmony with God. God's wisdom lived out by us results in a gentleness characterized by peacemaking, a humble learner's spirit, and active mercy. We will refuse to show favoritism, and we will instead demonstrate sincerity to all people.

8. Consider the same conflict you identified in question 6. How did your responses shape your reputation before others?

9. a. In what areas would God have you to rejoice in His work in your life—either because of your obedience or because of His loving revelation of your sin to you?

b. What would He want you to do now?

Reminder to Pray

Paul also reminded the Philippians that God wanted them to turn from anxiety to thankful prayer. Paul called the Philippians to earnestly seek God in prayer. He instructed them to bring their concerns to God with thankful hearts.

In conflict, we should first turn to God in prayer and share our hearts with Him. We can do this with thanksgiving when we anticipate what God will do in us as we trust in Him and respond obediently—when we prize lasting holiness more than fleeting happiness.

10. What warnings related to prayer did James give in James 4:1–14?

James knew people well. Our prayers reflect the desires of our hearts, and when we make our will the goal, our prayers become the means by which we attempt to get our own way. Great danger exists when we seek to use God to get our way. If we fail to see this sin and turn from it, our faith will erode because we will believe that God has failed to answer our prayers—that He is not trustworthy. In addition, we may mistake our own self-effort to bring about our will as the blessing of God on our lives. Instead, God calls on us to come to Him with open hands, thankful for His work in our lives, humbly bringing our requests to Him.

11. When you are in a conflict, what do you pray? Consider your prayers in the light of what we have studied.

12. In the midst of conflict, what should you pray for yourself? for others? Make a list of prayer requests that reflect a desire for the spiritual growth of everyone involved.

Look back at your prayer requests. God delights to answer requests for spiritual growth made humbly by His children. God answers these requests with growth that produces peace. Have you noticed what Paul promised to the Philippians as they responded to the conflict between Euodias and Syntyche in the ways he had described? He promised God's peace—a sense of being settled and put together in the midst of all circumstances. When we seek peace in our own way and for our own benefit, peace often eludes us; but when we submit ourselves to God's work in our lives, we will rest as He continues His work of conforming us to the image of His Son.

Sacrifices of Praise

13. Read Hebrews 13:15 and 16. What do these verses call on you to do?

Do you see the themes of Paul's writing in Philippians reflected in these verses from Hebrews? We offer words of sacrifice every time we speak. Our actions become our sacrifices offered in His presence. Sometimes our words and actions are a disgrace to Him. At other times, our words and actions offered in sacrifice to Him through rejoicing, through gentleness, and through thankful prayer bring glory to Him.

14. a. What types of sacrifices have you been bringing to God in the midst of conflict?

b. In what areas is He pleased with your sacrifices? Rejoice.

c. In what areas do you need to begin to offer pleasing sacrifices?

LESSON 6
WHAT MUST I DO?

After church your friend Trent gets your attention from across the auditorium and motions for you to join him in a quiet spot toward the front. As you approach him, you notice he seems distraught. Trent looks intently at you and says, "My son and I have not been getting along too well recently. This morning we exchanged some angry words on the way to church. This is really hard for me to admit, but I think I need some help to know how to respond to Tim."

"What can I do to help?" you reply tentatively.

Trent quickly responds, "You don't know this, but I have been watching you and your son. You seem to get along so well. I want you to help me. I want to learn from your example and have you teach me how to respond to my son the way you respond to yours."

After a moment of hesitation you reply, "Well, Trent, what you see here at church may not be the whole story. My son and I certainly have our moments. But, Trent, I do want to help you. Tell me about this morning; then let's pray together and set aside time this week to meet for coffee and more conversation."

1. As you consider the situation described above, what are you thinking? If this scenario had really happened, what fears would you have? In what areas would you find yourself rejoicing?

2. Based on this study of Philippians thus far, what do you think you would consider saying to Trent if you met for coffee?

3. Read the verses noted below and summarize the truths found in them.

Philippians 4:9

Philippians 3:17

Paul gave the Philippians some specific commands—instructing them in their responses to life, especially to the conflict between Euodias and Syntyche—but don't you expect there to be more? I do. Yet after these few commands we have studied, Paul ended his instruction with a simple injunction. In a sense he said to the Philippians, "Do what you know to do based on the instruction you have already received from me and based on the example that I have been to you."

Why might it be that Paul ended his instruction here? First, this simple instruction reflects Paul's emphasis on the Philippians' heart attitudes in the midst of conflict. When, by faith, a believer makes Christlikeness his or her goal, actions change to harmonize with that goal. After all, Christ told the Pharisees, "Cleanse first that which is within the cup and platter, that the outside of them may be clean also" (Matthew 23:26). Second, the record we have of Paul's instruction to and example before the Philippians provides a rather comprehensive look into the matters of obedience Paul was calling for in the Philippians' lives. In this lesson we will examine Paul's instructions that relate to conflict. In the final lesson, we will consider Paul's example.

Paul's Prayer

4. Consider Paul's prayer in Philippians 1:3–11. How does this instruction in prayer challenge your thinking, especially when you consider it in the light of the conflicts of life?

As the Philippians considered Paul's direction to follow his instruction and example, the confidence and content of Paul's prayer should have captured their attention. First, Paul's prayer for the Philippians was borne along by his confidence in God to complete His work in them. Conflicts are not a break in the action of God's gracious work of sanctification in our lives; they are a part of it, even a significant part. Paul demonstrated this confidence in God's ever-active, ever-faithful work through his faithful, confident prayers of thankfulness for the Philippians.

Second, when Paul prayed, he prayed for an inner change in the Philippians. His prayer instructed them to desire a love for

Christ and for one another that would result in discernment. This discernment would produce a tested purity and stability demonstrated by the Philippians' righteous living until the return of Christ.

Paul's prayer for the Philippians instructed them and us to trust God's work in us and to respond in love. His prayer reminds us that conflicts provide us with opportunities to sharpen our love for Christ and our love for others. This love sharpened on the whetstone of conflict then contributes to our own integrity and stability, resulting in an increased capacity to live out the righteousness of Christ.

5. a. In what areas do you see, or have you seen, God at work in the midst of your conflicts?

b. How has God used conflict to change you for His glory?

6. Read Philippians 1:27–30.

a. What instruction did Paul give in these verses that would help the Philippians to respond correctly to the conflict between Euodias and Syntyche?

b. How would this instruction challenge and provide direction to Euodias and Syntyche?

Worthy of the Gospel

Paul called on the Philippians to conduct themselves in a manner worthy of the gospel. In the gospel, the Philippians' enmity with God found its answer—once enemies of God, now sons; once strangers, now joint heirs. In the gospel, the Philippians had found the power to stand together with one purpose—once enemies, now brothers and sisters, once strangers now fellow pilgrims.

This instruction to live out the realities of the gospel carries with it a wonderful promise that also sounds a somber warning. When the Philippians stood together on the gospel, they would have the ability to stand against the attacks of those who would seek to draw them away from Christ.

Some conflicts must remain conflicts this side of Glory. God's plan never includes making peace with the enemies of the Cross. When God's people fail to respond to conflicts with the unity and steadfastness produced by the gospel, they run the risk of being terrified into surrender to the enemies of their souls. However, when motivated by the gospel, God's children turn obediently toward Christ and one another. God then uses this unity to remind the enemies of the Cross of their future destruction. This same obedient unity reminds Christ's brothers and sisters that the suffering they experience at the hands of His enemies will end when they fully and finally share in His victory.

7. Consider a recent conflict in which all the parties involved ultimately responded in ways that pleased Christ. How did God use this experience to strengthen your relationship with Him and others?

8. In what way did this experience or could this experience provide both a testimony to and protection from the enemies of the Cross?

The Mind of Christ

9. Read the following passages. What instruction did Paul give, and how did this instruction provide direction to believers in the midst of conflict?

> Philippians 2:1–5

> Philippians 2:14–16

Paul pleaded with the Philippians to respond to Christ's work in them by seeking to live according to the mind of Christ. We considered these verses in the first lesson, but take a moment to consider them once again. Self-promotion and division may prove effective in winning elections, but they never please Christ. Looking out for Number One may result in personal power and affluence, but it never exhibits the humility of Christ. Complaining and selfish deliberation may relieve personal tension, but they always tarnish the glass through which the light of Christ should shine unhindered.

In conflict, we must seek to lift up Christ. His goals and priorities must be ours. His humility must live in us through the energy of His Spirit. We must fix our attention on the good of others and the glory of Christ. We must fight our natural sinful tendencies to speak divisive words of murmur and complaint, and instead we must speak words that reflect our position as children of God—words that draw people's attention to Christ. Once again, when we speak and act in ways that honor Christ, not only do we promote Christ-centered, other-focused unity, we also live lives that clearly hold out the light of Christ for our entire world to see.

10. Consider your words and actions in a recent conflict. Where did they reflect selfishness and pride? Confess these sins to God. Turn to Him for the strength to speak words of Christlike humility.

11. a. In what ways did your words reflect love for Christ and others?

b. In what ways has God used this experience in your life and the lives of others?

Discernment and Vigilance

12. Read Philippians 3:1–3. What does this passage teach you about conflicts and Paul's instruction concerning a believer's response?

Paul addressed two serious conflicts in the book of Philippians. The conflict within the church between Euodias and Syntyche and the conflict from outside the church in which false teachers sought to draw the Philippians away from Christ. Paul called on the Philippians to solve the conflict between Euodias and Syntyche by striving to become of the same mind in the Lord. The resultant unity would help them to stand firm against the conflict from the outside.

Paul instructed the Philippians to respond to the attack from the outside, not by resolving differences with the enemy, but by seeing the enemy through discerning eyes. These eyes of discernment would then lead the Philippians to refuse to give in to the temptation to follow the false teachers, and instead, to follow after those whose teaching and lives reflected Christ.

In the midst of conflicts, we must always be willing to give up our rights and our ways, but we must never be willing to give up God's will and way. Have you noticed that Paul's instruction to the Philippians continually emphasized this distinction? Conflicts call us to vigilance—vigilance to stand up against our own sinful desires and vigilance to stand against those who stand against Christ. Without this vigilance, harm will come to us and to our brothers and sisters in Christ.

13. Read Philippians 3:20 and 21.

    a. What truths in these verses can help you face conflicts?

    b. How can these truths reorient your priorities?

14. As you have faced conflict, in what area have you been tempted to turn your back on God's will and way?

When Paul called on the Philippians to practice what they

had learned from him, he called them to rely on rich teaching that connected Christ's character and work to *their* character and responses. When Paul called on them to follow his example, he called on them to see Christ at work in him. Paul's confident appeal to act on his teaching and follow his example was embedded in his confidence in the work Christ was doing in his own life. The work also took place in the lives of the Philippians. And this work takes place in us as we submit ourselves to Christ and allow His Spirit to work in us.

15. Consider how Christ has changed you in the past through the vehicle of conflicts. How is He continuing to shape you into His image?

LESSON 7
WHO ARE MY EXAMPLES?

Several years ago we experienced a major blizzard. The snow came down so quickly and the wind blew with such force that we could not see from our front door to the street less than one hundred feet away. After the snow stopped and the wind died down, the real work began. Living in a duplex at the time, I shared the snow-removal task with my neighbor. Both of us went out into the snow and fought against the drifts in the driveway with our shovels. It felt like a losing battle.

As my neighbor and I took a brief break, leaning on our shovels, his front door opened and out came a three-foot bundle of snow boots, snow pants, a winter coat, mittens, and a scarf. Somewhere inside all of that winter garb was my neighbor's son. Because of the protective clothing, that otherwise slender boy was almost as wide as he was tall.

Since my neighbor and I had begun our shoveling in the driveway, the sidewalk was still covered in over two feet of snow.

We watched the little lad carefully follow his daddy's footprints in the snow so that he could come and help us with his little shovel. His plan worked, and he was tackling the mountains of snow. But then it happened. He missed one footprint, then another, and in one quick moment, he found himself buried up to his neck in snow. In an instant that probably seemed like an eternity to that snowbound child, his father scooped him into his arms and sat him safely on the partially shoveled driveway.

Following in Someone's Footprints

As we find our way through the difficulties of this life, we often feel as if we are trapped in a snowbank. Yet we are never fully and finally trapped. Why? Because our Savior has walked the path before us and now He walks with us. Brothers and sisters in Christ have walked before us, and we are walking with other brothers and sisters in Christ.

Example holds tremendous authority over us. We always follow someone's example. This reality drove Paul to remind the Philippians to follow his example carefully because they had seen him follow Christ. Following Christ's example and the examples of those who follow Christ provides protection and direction in the midst of life's conflicts.

1. a. Whose example do you follow? Where do you turn for advice in conflict?

  b. Consider your examples (from question 1a). Do these people point you to Christ or away from Him?

2. Read Acts 16:11–40. What lessons can you learn from Paul's response to the beating he received in Philippi?

3. a. If you had witnessed this event, how do you think it might have influenced you?

b. How should it influence you today?

From the very beginning, the Philippians had seen how Paul had handled conflict. He lived as a godly example. His life was consistent with his message. In the persecution described here in Acts, Paul taught the Philippians by example what he taught them to do by his instruction. The principles Paul taught the Philippians were true because they came from God. The principles Paul taught them were credible because Paul lived them out in his life.

Responsibility to Others

Notice how Paul's example reflected his teaching. Paul and his fellow travelers made it their goal to honor God and become like Christ. Their relationship with God and their responsibility to others governed their responses in the midst of this conflict. Paul and Silas patiently endured for God's glory. They rejoiced and sang praises, not because they loved suffering, but because they loved God and interpreted their lives and circumstances from His perspective. They also viewed others from God's perspective. This perspective drove their gentle, obedient responses to the jailer who just hours before had carelessly and roughly bound them in the deepest part of the prison. This Spirit-produced gentleness resulted in the salvation of the jailer and the individuals of his household.

Even Paul and Silas's refusal to leave prison provided an example and ongoing protection for the Philippians and contributed to their protection. If they had chosen their own will, Paul and Silas might have interpreted their release as an opportunity to get out of town without running the risk of further mistreatment. Yet Paul and Silas stood up to those who had beaten them so they would have an opportunity to comfort the new believers. Paul and Silas's actions toward those who beat them also likely protected the new believers from ongoing persecution. The city leaders would never risk the loss of power that would result if word of their misstep ever reached Rome. The penalty for such gross mismanagement—occupation by Roman troops—would far outweigh any benefit received from persecuting the new believers.

We, too, must follow Paul's example. We can obey God in the midst of conflict because God works in us. We can find hope that energizes us to obey because we have seen God work in Paul. We can find determination to obey because we have seen God at work in other brothers and sisters in Christ.

4. How do the examples of Paul and Silas give you hope to face the conflicts of life?

5. How has God used others to give you hope in the midst of conflict?

6. Read Philippians 1:12–18. How did Paul's response to those who preached the gospel in Rome provide an example for the Philippians to follow in conflict?

Furthering the Gospel

As Paul offered a brief report of his imprisonment, he demonstrated amazing love for the gospel and for the God of the gospel. Paul described the advancement of the gospel that had taken place as result of his arrest. His confinement resulted in Christ's becoming known throughout the headquarters of the governor of Rome. Paul's faithful witness during his imprisonment gave hope to other believers, encouraging them to share the gospel. Many people preached the gospel from pure hearts motivated by love for Christ and an understanding that Paul's unjust imprisonment provided a potent defense of the gospel—a defense that demonstrated its power and validity. Some, however, found their boldness to preach the gospel from hearts motivated by their own desire for position and power. Paul did not condone this motive—after all, he took the time to point it out. Neither did Paul allow himself to become sidetracked in his walk with God in the context of others' sins. He rejoiced that the work of the gospel of Christ moved forward.

Notice again how Paul's example reflected his message. Faced with the possible close of his ministry on earth, Paul did not try—even for a moment—to remake the message of the gospel into a message about his glory and kingdom. Rather, he demonstrated that he believed that the gospel is about God's glory and His church. Because Paul fixed his attention on God's glory, he interpreted his situation from God's perspective. He was not naïve. At the same time, he did not turn his attention to himself. His attitude and his subsequent response gave Paul cause for rejoicing in Christ and in the furtherance of Christ's message.

In the energy of Christ, we can follow Paul's example. As we make God's goal our goal, we will interpret ourselves, others, and our circumstances from God's point of view. We will respond obediently, rejoicing in God's work in us and through us in the face of conflict.

7. Read Philippians 3:4–14. How did Paul provide an example to follow through this contrast of himself with the false teachers who threatened the Philippians' unity?

Review

To protect the Philippians from the false teachers who threatened to shake their faith, Paul rehearsed God's gracious work in his life. As you read Paul's testimony and commitment to press on in ministry, did you see all of the themes we have studied together lived out in his life? Paul learned the lesson and lived out the truth that life is about Christ. Paul desired Christ, and he lived from Christ's perspective. From this way of making sense out of his life, Paul gave himself to loving others. His obedience to Christ's work in him made him a worthy, credible example for the Philippians to follow.

8. As we close our study, consider the aspects of Paul's example we have studied together. How does Paul's example instruct and challenge you to follow the themes Paul emphasized with the Philippians in the midst of the conflict between Euodias and Syntyche?

How does Paul's example instruct and challenge you to do the following:
- ❏ Make God's glory and your own growth in Christlikeness your goal in the midst of conflict.
- ❏ Remind yourself of the character and work of your God in ways that draw your attention away from yourself to Him.
- ❏ View others as God views them and claim His standard of evaluation, His Word, as your own.
- ❏ Think thoughts that reflect the character of God and love for others, seeking to view yourself, others, and your circumstances from His perspective.
- ❏ Obey Paul's commands to rejoice, to cultivate a reputation of gentleness, and to turn from anxiety to thankful prayer.
- ❏ Do what you know you should do on the basis of the Biblical instruction you have received.
- ❏ Follow the examples of others who follow Christ and become a Christlike example to others.

And finally, rejoice in these words from Paul: "Wherefore, my beloved, as ye have always obeyed, not as in my presence only, but now much more in my absence, work out your own salvation with fear and trembling. For it is God which worketh in you both to will and to do of his good pleasure" (Philippians 2:12, 13).

His work takes place every moment—even in the moments, days, week, months, and years of conflict. Because God works, we can obey and see God bring our salvation to its goal—our conformity to the glorious image of His Son. Imagine it! He works in you every moment to help you look more and more like a member of His family.

Afterword

Thank you for taking the time to study this material. In writing it, I have prayed that it would help you, the reader, see Christ as actively involved in every part of your life. I have prayed that this realization would motivate you in the energy of His Spirit to respond to conflicts in ways that would result in Christ's glory and your growth.

The Bible speaks richly to the particulars of our lives. I trust that this study has helped you to more fully realize this fact and to rejoice in it more deeply.

In writing this material, I also recognize that conflicts happen in specific and sometimes puzzling detail. At times throughout the study, you may have found yourself struggling to connect what Paul was teaching to the details of a conflict you have had or are experiencing.

Please allow me to encourage you. God has given you the gift of your pastor to help you connect the truths of the Scriptures to these details of your life. Please contact him and invite him to spend some time with you, or let him direct you to another brother or sister in Christ who can help you. God never leaves His people without the resources they need to respond obediently to Him. You are not alone in the midst of the conflicts that come as you live before God in this fallen, broken world. Christ lives in you, and brothers and sisters in Christ walk with you.

ANSWERS

Lesson 1

4. Fulfill, or complete, Paul's joy by becoming like-minded.

5. By not acting in selfishness or pride, by humbly considering others more important than themselves, and by concerning themselves with the welfare of others.

8. (a) Have the mind of Christ—humility. (b) Paul wanted Euodias and Syntyche to be of the same mind in the Lord. If the women possessed the humble mind of Christ, they would be of the same mind in the Lord.

9. *Characteristic*—Christ's humility. *Works*—Jesus demonstrated this humility by leaving Heaven to come to earth, by becoming fully man while remaining fully God, by living the life of a servant, and by submitting Himself to the death of the cross.

10. Those who meet their trials and temptations with humble obedience are promised the crown of life. They are also promised growth in patience and spiritual maturity through the process.

13. Answers might include the following: believers' relationships with one another, Paul's love and concern for the Philippians, the command to be of the same mind in the Lord, the command to help Euodias and Syntyche, the command to rejoice, the command to be gentle toward others, the peace of God, the command to turn from anxiety to prayer, the command for believers to control their thoughts, and the command to follow the example and instruction of Paul.

Lesson 2

3. Paul emphasized the women's relationship to each other and their relationship to God.

5. *Verse 1*—God provides the ability to stand fast. *Verse 2*—God provides the ability to be of the same mind. *Verse 4*—God is the source and person of rejoicing. *Verse 5*—God is near, and His Son

may return at any moment. *Verse 6*—God hears the prayers of His children. *Verses 7, 9*—God is the source of peace.

7.

Passage	Picture	Focus	God's Stability
Psalm 18:1–3	Strength, rock, fortress, deliverer, buckler (shield), horn of salvation, and high tower (stronghold).	Personal answers.	Personal answers.
Psalm 95:1–7	Rock of my salvation, a great God, and a great King. He is the creator and sustainer. He created us, and we are His people.	Personal answers.	Personal answers.
Proverbs 30:5	A shield to those who trust Him.	Personal answers.	Personal answers.
Romans 12:16–21	The avenger of His people.	Personal answers.	Personal answers.

8. *Psalm 133:1–3*—It is good and pleasant for brothers to live together in unity. *Romans 12:9–21*—Unity grows in the midst of people of good character. Unity grows when love and humility are present. Unity grows when people serve the Lord and each other. Unity grows when people bless those who curse them. Unity grows when people rejoice and weep together. Unity grows when people seek to become of the same mind. Unity grows when people seek to live peaceably. Unity grows when people trust God to be their avenger. Unity grows when people serve their enemies. *Ephesians 4:1–16*—Humility, meekness, and forbearance result in Spirit-produced unity and peace. God has provided a foundation for unity through one body, one Spirit, one hope, One Lord, one faith, one baptism, and One Father.

12. The presence of God provides contentment, rest, provision, strength, and direction. The presence of God provides peace and comfort in the midst of life's dark valleys. The presence of God provides us with bountiful provision in the face of opposition. Goodness

and mercy accompany the presence of God. His presence is always with the believer, and someday each believer will live forever in His presence.

13. Christ's presence—His look at Peter—caused Peter to weep bitterly over his sin.

15. (a) God's peace that surpasses understanding will guard our hearts and minds through Christ. (b) The God of peace Himself will be with us when we take our anxieties to Him.

16. Conflicts come from our lusts—our strong desires—that fight for control of us. (Which do we want more: God's way or ours—to be obedient to Him, or to get what we want?)

17. We must submit to God and resist the Devil. When we draw close to God, He will draw close to us. We must cleanse our actions ("hands") and our motives ("hearts").

Lesson 3

1. As his brethren, dearly beloved, longed for, joy and crown, and yokefellow; as women who labored with him in the gospel; as his fellow laborers; as people whose names are in the Book of Life.

3.

Passage	What You Can Learn
Galatians 6:1, 2	Believers have a responsibility for each other's spiritual well-being.
Philippians 1:12–18	Believers have a common mission. Believers influence each other by their examples.
2 Thessalonians 3:11–16	Believers have a responsibility to warn erring brothers in love and separate from them if they refuse to submit to God's Word.
Philemon 10–21	Believers are to encourage one another toward love and good works.

4.

Passages	Writer's Message	Readers' Reception
2 Corinthians 7:1	Live pure and holy lives in the fear of God.	They probably sensed both Paul's concern for them and the seriousness of the command and responded positively.
Philippians 2:12–16	Actively work out your salvation in humble submission to God's work in you.	They likely caught Paul's deeply personal commitment to their spiritual growth and readily received his message.
2 Peter 3:1–4, 13–18	Avoid falling into error by growing in the grace and knowledge of Jesus Christ.	Peter's personal desire for them to avoid error and grow should have motivated them to respond in obedience.

7. (a) He called them carnal. (b) He exposed their errors by describing for them the envy, strife, and divisions that resulted from their failure to resolve their conflict. He taught them the truth about himself as a servant of God, about God as the One Who gives the increase, and about themselves as God's field and God's building.

8. Possible answers include the following: Paul called his readers to resolve their conflict in a Christlike manner. Paul called on his readers to see God, themselves, and others from God's perspective. Paul refocused his readers' attention on God and the relationship they shared with each other, based on their relationship with God.

9. *Revelation 20:11–15*—Those individuals whose names are not found written in the Book of Life will be cast into the Lake of Fire. *Revelation 21:10–27*—Those individuals whose names are written in the Book of Life will share the presence and blessings of God forever.

10. Every individual is created in the image ("similitude") of God.

11. *1 John 2:1, 2*—Christ is the propitiation (satisfaction) for the sins of all mankind. *2 Peter 2:1*—Christ died for them (bought them).

Lesson 4

1. Paul commanded his readers to examine their thinking patterns and to intentionally direct and control them.

2. Abraham concluded that to obey God, he must sacrifice his son Isaac. Abraham also concluded that for God to keep His promises about Isaac, He would have to raise Isaac from the dead.

4. He needed to put the past behind him and reach forward. He needed to give his energy to loving and serving Christ.

6. Possible answers include the following: *True*—false, wrong. *Honest*—deceitful, dishonest, insincere. *Just*—unrighteous, unjust, wrong. *Pure*—defiled, impure, contaminated. *Lovely*—ugly, hateful, displeasing. *Of good report*—evil, wicked, false. *Virtuous*—depraved, evil, sinful. *Praiseworthy*—worthless, critical.

10. A variety of similarities exists between the characteristics of love given in 1 Corinthians 13 and the characteristics of thinking in Philippians 4:8. A few examples follow.

Characteristic in 1 Corinthians 13	Characteristic in Philippians 4:8
"Envieth not" (v. 4)	True, honest, just, lovely
"Seeketh not her own" (v. 4)	Lovely
"Is not puffed up" (v. 4)	True, honest
"Is kind" (v. 4)	Lovely
"Doth not behave itself unseemly" (v. 5)	Just
"Thinketh no evil" (v. 5)	Pure
"Rejoiceth not in iniquity" (v. 6)	Of good report, pure
"Rejoiceth in the truth" (v. 6)	True

14. *2 Corinthians 10:5*—Paul called his readers to take their thoughts captive and to break down thinking that is against the knowledge of God. *Matthew 6:34*—Christ called on His hearers to refuse to dwell on tomorrow, but rather to face today's problems and responsibilities. *Romans 12:3*—Paul instructed his readers to think humbly of themselves while relying on God's work in them.

Lesson 5

2. (a) My responses in the midst of conflict come out of my heart. (b) My words reflect the good or bad that is in my heart at the time I speak the words. (c) My heart must change if I am to respond to conflicts in a Christlike manner. (I must turn from my own desires and must desire to please Christ alone.)

3. Rejoice; let your moderation/gentleness be known to all; turn from anxiety to prayer.

4. We share in Christ's sufferings. We will respond with calm rejoicing because we are bringing glory to God and growing in our walk with Him.

5. God's chastening is evidence of His love for His children. God's chastening is evidence that we are His children. Our submissive response to God's chastening produces our growth in holiness, which results in peace.

7. Gentleness demonstrates a person's wisdom. God's wisdom is pure and peaceable. People who are wise before God will be gentle. They will be reasonable ("easy to be intreated"), "full of mercy and good fruits," stable, and "without hypocrisy." Their seeds of peace will bring forth the fruit of righteousness.

10. James warned against praying for our own desires to be fulfilled—to get our own way—in the midst of conflict. He warned against failing to pray with God's glory as our supreme concern.

13. These verses call on us to guard our words and actions and to offer them as sacrifices of praise to God because God is pleased by these types of sacrifices.

Lesson 6

3. *Philippians 4:9*—Paul wanted his readers to follow his instruction and his example. As a result, they would experience God's peace. *Philippians 3:17*—Paul instructed his readers to follow his example and the example of others who lived godly lives.

6. (a) Paul called on the Philippians to conduct themselves in a manner worthy of the gospel. (b) When Euodias and Syntyche lived in this way, they would stand together and strive together for the gospel. This commitment to the gospel would protect them from the enemies of the gospel, and it would allow them to faithfully endure suffering for the cause of Christ. This instruction should have encouraged Euodias and Syntyche to follow Paul's instruction so that they could protect themselves from the attacks of those outside of Christ.

9. *Philippians 2:1–5*—Paul instructed the Philippians to be likeminded, to love each other, to be united in purpose and mind. He warned them against strife and pride and called them to humility. He instructed them to imitate the humility of Christ. *Philippians 2:14–16*—Paul called on the believers to refuse murmuring, complaining, and arguing. Paul reminded the Philippians that if they refused such actions, they would be individuals of integrity who effectively hold forth the gospel to others. This instruction calls believers to look away from themselves and to focus on loving others and glorifying God.

12. We are to be aware of the enemies of God. We cannot make peace or resolve conflicts when to do so would compromise the truth. We must trust God and not ourselves.

13. (a) We are citizens of Heaven, and we should look for the return of Christ. When He comes, He will change us to be like Him. The conflicts of this life are temporary. (b) These truths should motivate us to live for Christ's glory and resist the temptation to fear others. As a result, we will refuse to compromise the truth for the sake of a false peace.

Lesson 7

2. Some possible answers include the following: I can learn to care for the souls of others, make it my goal to please and glorify God, endure persecution for God's glory, praise God in the midst of conflict and persecution, respond with gentle concern for the eternal

destiny of others as Paul did for the jailer and his family, give comfort to other believers—new believers—in the midst of my own mistreatment and suffering.

6. Paul's love for God and his concern for the spread of the gospel were more important to Paul than his personal mistreatment. Even though some preached the gospel with a desire to add to Paul's suffering, Paul still rejoiced that the gospel was being preached. If the Philippians followed his example, they would rejoice in the spreading of the gospel and would endure suffering on behalf of the gospel.

7. To serve Christ, Paul gave up all of the things of his former life that might have provided him with power and prestige. He made Christ and His teachings central to his life and ministry. In contrast, the false teachers made themselves and their teachings the center of attention.